A Heart on Fire

Poems
from
the Flames

David C. Weiss

ISBN 978-1-938883-85-9

Designed and produced by
Maine Authors Publishing
558 Main Street
Rockland, Maine 04841
www.maineauthorspublishing.com

Printed in the United States of America

This book is dedicated to my sons Matthew and Adam

and to the children of Heart House, 1945–1947.

Acknowledgments

I am grateful to my mentor, Ruth Townsend Story, who encouraged and sustained me in writing my poems with her patience, skill, and kindness as well as her enthusiasm and playfulness.

I am thankful for the members of Maine Authors Publishing who shepherded this book through the publishing process with their artistry and patience, especially Lindy Gifford, Cheryl McKeary, Nikki Giglia, and Genie Daley.

In the stillness of the quiet, if we listen, we can hear the whisper of the heart giving strength to weakness, courage to fear, hope to despair.

Howard Thurman, Past Dean of Marsh Chapel, Boston University

Foreword

Two events in my childhood have served as emotional and spiritual templates for my life. I teetered on the threshold of death in both experiences, which, as an adult, I have come to believe were imbued with the numinous presence of God.

The first episode occurred when I was age five and contracted rheumatic fever, which affected my heart. After a brief hospitalization, I was separated from my family and lived for two years in a facility called Heart House in Valencia, Pennsylvania, a medical home for children recovering from heart disorders. I lived at Heart House from 1945 to 1947.

The second experience was at age eleven, when I was hospitalized for three months with another heart infection, which again brought me to death's door. Through the skill and care of my doctors and loving support of my parents, my fragile heart recovered.

My heart grew stronger during my teenage years, and I was able to participate in competitive sports such as swimming. Now, at age seventy-three, there is a whisper of a murmur in my heart indicating that it has not completely healed, remembering how close I came to dying as a young boy.

Each beat of my heart is a moment of grace and a reminder of how precious and vulnerable is life. I try to live each day with an open heart—as if it has been cured in God's furnace and has been set on fire with love and gratefulness.

Whatever your affliction, may these poems help ignite a healing fire in your heart.

David C. Weiss

God's Furnace

Your command erupts from the fire
like molten steel surging from a foundry furnace:

"Step into the flames.
I will set your heart on fire."

As I take the first step, the inferno begins
to dissolve the armor around my heart

like lead transforming into gold
in the alchemist's furnace.

God's Finger

When God's finger lightly pressed against my chest

like a candle lighting another candle,

my spirit began to glow with gratitude.

Doubts

What is this fire burning within me?

Is it dry tinder within my heart
set ablaze by a spark from You?

Is the heat of Your fiery love seeking me?

Breathe unceasingly on the embers of my heart,
for my doubts want to extinguish Your flame.

Surrender

Come Holy Spirit,

break open the armor of my heart;

help it throb with courage

to be vulnerable to love.

Lord, I Pray…

Let my ears hear what You hear.

Let my eyes see what You see.

Let my lips say what You say.

Let my breath be what You breathe.

Let my thinking be what You think.

Let my heart beat in harmony with Your heart,

of grace, compassion, and forgiveness.

What God Sees

I want to see what God sees

I want to see my soul before I was born

I want to see the moment of my creation

I want to see angels hovering around me as I die

I want to see them carry me into God's heart

Then I will see what God sees.

God's Hands

What are God's hands like?

Are they silky as a rose petal
or callused as a stone cutter's?

Are they soothing as a lover's caress
or searing as sun-soaked desert sand?

Still I long to be held in God's hands.

Hoping to Catch God

I am a salmon in a cascading stream,
stars piloting my way home.

I am a bee swarming with
my queen in a droning dervish.

I am a rainbow reflecting the radiance
of angels frolicking in a spring shower.

I am a butterfly creating galaxies
by fluttering my stardust-covered wings.

I am a spider weaving a gossamer web
anchored to stars,
hoping to catch God.

Where God Is

God is everywhere and nowhere.

Cease searching for Her.

You cannot find Her.

Be still, be silent,

And She will find you.

Unlatch the Door

Ancient Love is knocking at my heart's door.

Love says, "Will you unlatch the door and invite me to enter?"

I answer, "Once, you came into my tent of affliction,
then disappeared leaving bloodstains in your wake."

Love says, "When you were a child, I held you in my bosom
and soothed your scarred heart."

I ask, "Are you here with your balm only to leave again?"

Love answers, "Your fear banished me. I am standing at your door
waiting to be invited in."

I ask, "What is it I fear?"

Love says, "Being vulnerable to love."

Angels in a Restaurant

An elderly man and woman sit in a restaurant;
the woman focuses on a plate of meatloaf and gravy
oozing over a mountain of mashed potatoes,
the man gazes at the ceiling, a fork in hand
gesturing as if forming images in the air.

If you peer into his thick-lens glasses,
do you fear being infected by the loneliness behind his moist eyes?

Can you recall when you last kissed his parched lips?

Do you remember her arthritic fingers clasping your trembling hand
as you stood next to your mother's breathless body?

When did you cease listening to her monologue of swollen ankles,
aching joints, her dearest friend listed in the morning obituaries?

Can you remember when you last touched her taut face?

When was the last time you said you loved one another?

What unspoken grief imprisons you in adjoining cells?

Look up. See the face of the angel sitting across from you.

As She Sees It

If I look through the eyes of my beloved

and envision the world as she sees it,

will I witness the tragedy of Shakespeare's *Hamlet*

or the comedy of Woody Allen's *Sleeper*?

God's Bees

Loving kindness is like a field of wildflowers

whose nectar is carried by God's bees

to the honeycomb of our heart.

Gifts of God

In the muted light of a chapel
a small boy stands beneath the altar

his eyes fixed on a painting
of the child Jesus reaching toward him.

The boy extends his hand as if
recognizing each other as gifts of God.

Room Labeled Grief

Orpheus voyaged to the netherworld
to rescue his dead wife Eurydice,
commanded by the gods not to look back at her
until they reached the world of the living.

But Orpheus looked back,
and Eurydice vanished for a second time,
forever.

The gods gave Orpheus a chance
to escape the despair of losing Eurydice,
but like mortals, Orpheus had to wrap
the cloak of grief around his stricken heart
and mourn his beloved.

Lost love finds a home in our hearts forever,
but only after we have slept in a room labeled "Grief."

On Losing a Friend

In your twenty-second year, the sickle of death

laid claim to your emaciated body as cancer

swept in like a hungry bear with its horny nails

tearing at your body and my already grieving heart.

Memories offer no solace to my longing for you.

Necessary Grief

Sometimes I believe my grief is singular,
as if I am the only wave hurled
against that craggy coast.

Trying to find comfort,
I recall the story of the Buddha
and a grieving mother.

Buddha said he would resurrect her son
if she could find a home in her village
where no one had died.

Later she returned to the Buddha
and said, "I understand."
Then went to bury her child.

Knowing that others suffer losses
helps me bury my dead,
but does not assuage my grief.

Windows

I see Your face in the eyes
of the poor, the hungry, the infirm.

I see Your face in the eyes of the homeless
begging for change on a street corner.

I see Your face in the eyes of my beloved
grieving the loss of our passion.

Does she see Your face in my eyes
reflecting heartbreak?

Grieving Brothers

Are you afraid to reveal your sorrow
as we stand next to our brother's casket?

Is your heart caught off guard
as I drape my arm over your shoulder?

Your body becomes rigid like drying concrete.

You move away as if yanking a dressing
from an unhealed wound.

Was your mourning too unbearable
to allow my affection to touch your heartache?

You turn and walk away.

I grieve the loss of another brother.

Transformation

I am a snowflake birthed in wintry darkness,

a nascent droplet refashioned by temperature
into a feathery crystal,

twirling, whirling, floating,

finally grounded with other snowy angels
forming a mantle of white stillness,

reflecting the blue-gray lunar face of God.

Dreams

Mystics say dreams are sent from God

to shepherd our souls home

like butterflies migrating by stars at night.

Questions for a Monarch

Your black, white, and yellow body
crawls slowly, deliberately, along the surface of the leaf,
head bobbing, mandible munching semicircles
along the edge of the milkweed blade.

Do you know of the oyamel fir that awaits you
as you attach yourself to a branchlet
and begin to ooze a gossamer veil around your fuzzy body?

Does your spinning portend death
as you curl your body upward and exude
the final thread of your silky shroud?

Are you aware of the adventure that summons you?

Do you feel the force trembling within the membranes of your cells
that will set you on the path of becoming a king?

Can you refuse to knit your chrysalis of kingly potential,
content to live a brief life on a milky weed?

Perhaps you have no choice but to surrender
to the wild urge within you.

Will I go so instinctively, so willingly?
Do I have the courage to spin
a chrysalis at my final breath
and step across the threshold that separates
my soul from its regal inheritance?

Am I willing to weave that final silky thread
around my earthly frame and morph into a winged creature
soaring with other monarchs to my royal home?

Turning Over the Reins

Helios steers his sun chariot daily east to west across the cerulean sky.
His son Phaethon pleads to pilot alone his father's majestic carriage.

Helios, wanting to protect his son, warns that not even Zeus,
the supreme god and protector of humankind, would dare to drive it,
as the chariot is fiery hot and the horses breathe out flames.
But Phaethon is adamant and Helios reluctantly hands him the reins.

Phaethon gives a quick snap to the restraints and the immortal steeds
lunge forward, obediently continuing their solar orbit.

But Phaethon cannot restrain the power of his father's horses,
plunging the chariot and rider toward earth.

Zeus, sensing the danger, hurls a thunderbolt, slaying Phaethon,
saving earth, and preserving the fiery carriage to continue
its unalterable journey across the sky.

Like Helios, I tried to protect my son from hazarding himself
in the world, fearing cosmic forces would plunge him to earth.

But unlike Phaethon, he harnessed the power of his impulsiveness,
now coursing his own orbit, bringing joy to his father's heart.

Words to Live By

"What words do you live by?"
a father asks his son.

"Wisdom and compassion," he says.

"What words do you live by?"
a son asks his father.

"Kindness and patience," he says.

Their words weave a silken cloak
from the looms of their hearts,
healing the breach between them.

Shadows

The three of us pose in a photo memorializing
my spiritual confirmation in the Lutheran Church.

My mother on my right, Father on my left.
I'm the thirteen-year-old boy wedged between them
as if a slight shift of their bodies toward the center
would make me to disappear.

Mother and I look into the camera, Father gazes off to his left.
June sun casts shadows below our squinting eyes and
shields our vulnerability from the camera's lens.

Mother's face reflects stoic acceptance,
Father's mouth hints a wary smile.
A forced grin belies my anxiety.

Mother wears a short-sleeved, frayed dress,
one hand snuggled in her right torn pocket,
her hair bobby-pinned behind each ear.

Father's white shirt open at the collar,
dark rumpled pants held up by a belt
below a protruding stomach.
He clasps a bottle of beer in his left hand,
extended away from his side, an attempt
to hide it from the camera's eye.
His right arm around the back of my head,
his hand rests on my mother's left shoulder.
I wear a suit, white shirt, and narrow tie.
A white carnation on my left lapel,
its fragile edges crumpling against my father's side.

Does the camera's lens discern that I am the lapel flower,
crushed between my father's unpredictable rage
and my mother's despair?

Is the camera able to sound us, as in navigation,
to plumb the hidden depth of our love?

Dear Mother, Dear Father:

I forgive you for not being
the parents I wanted you to be.

Dear Son:

We forgive you for not being
the son we hoped you would be.

Father, 1917

I find your face in the sepia image
sitting in the front row, far right, your white shirt
cuffed at the wrist, complete with a borrowed tie,
hands obediently resting on your gray knickers
gathered at the top of your knee-length socks,
thick brown leather shoes,
your light brown hair parted from left to right.

Do your dreams portend the heartaches that lie in wait for you:
a home with thirteen children; scarcity of food; poverty of affection;
a younger brother and sister succumbing to the flu epidemic;
a hard-hearted father; an exhausted mother;
your lifelong struggle with depression and alcoholism.

I want to reach into the picture to touch your expressionless face
and wrap my arms around your small body to protect you
from the pain that will haunt your life.

I cannot rescue you from the darkness that awaits
or prevent my living under the shadow of your despair.

Why I Don't Go to Cocktail Parties

Cocktail parties are filled with prattle,
voices chortling like chickens in a barnyard,
blaring music stupefying the senses,

smiles frigid as dead birds in winter,
eyes play at listening as if watching a silent movie,
shallow, well-rehearsed responses as I stand

frozen, waiting to thaw and evaporate.

Seeds

Silence and stillness are seeds of God's grace

impregnating the womb of my soul,

bringing peace to my restive heart.

The Holy

You ask to witness the Holy:

Watch a mother nursing her infant,

Children sharing their lunch at school,

A father kissing his son,

A coin placed in the palm of a beggar,

A crocus blossom rising from thawed earth.

See, you *can* witness the Holy.

Unhindered

A pure heart unhindered

by ego's demands and fears

is like a translucent diamond

reflecting the spectrum of God's love.

Soul's Holy Well

Unbridled avarice and disdain of the poor

are like acid leaching into a mother's milk,

contaminating the soul's holy well from which

are drawn the waters of grace and benevolence.

Riding the Back of a Tiger

I don't want to live my life
clutching the tail of a tiger.

I want to live riding on his back.
I want to hear his panting and snorting,
my body absorbing the collision of his paws
on the ground beneath us.

I want to feel the rhythmic contraction
of his haunches and smell
the scent of blood on his breath.

I want to vibrate with each gyration of his backbone,
and gaze into his narrow vertical pupils
to witness his vision in pursuing his prey.

This is how I want to live in the world:
riding the sleek body of a tiger,
soaking my senses with life's instinctual wildness,
and at the end of my untamable ride,
to dismount and be empowered by it.

Autumnal Dance

When I die, I want to be like a leaf
pirouetting to earth in a life-inspired autumnal dance.

I want to join the scuffing, whooshing chorus
of other fallen leaves as a breeze sweeps across
our amber-golden bodies, lifting us in a whirling dervish.

Our swirling playfulness wanes as a fading zephyr
tenderly cradles us to the damp earth.

Ashen blotches of mold will feed on our arid bodies.
Our once verdant faces will slowly blacken with the color of death.

Then Mother Earth will bury her dead
to morph into a nest of humus, incubate a single seed,
and birth another autumnal dance.

Last Day

Each morning, a Buddhist monk
asks an imaginary bird sitting on his shoulder:
"Is today the day I will die?"

The bird doesn't answer, its perching reminding
the monk to decide how he wants to live
his last day.

If today is the day I will die,
I want to write a poem,
send a silent blessing to two people quarreling on a street,
address by name a cashier at a grocery store,
express compassion to a despondent brother,
seek forgiveness from those I have grieved.

If I awake tomorrow, I'll ask the bird again.

Enough

When I despair about my future
I hear the Buddha say
all you need to know is *now*:

The redolence of a red rose
in the garden

Light glinting off dew-glazed needles
of an evergreen

A chipmunk scurrying
over sun-bathed summer grass

My cat Annie dutifully cleaning
her silky fur.

Be calm, restive heart,
and savor the *now*.

Hummingbird

I am a hummingbird in a dark room

wings quivering over my quickened heart

igniting a flame to light my way home.

Epitaph

A stone is rolled against the portal
of my heart's self-imposed exile.

Written across its face in dried blood is the epitaph:

"Here lies the body of a boy touched by God,
a secret he kept hidden within the caverns of his heart."

My lesioned heart has been cured in the infirmary
of God's love and there is a new epitaph:

"Here rests a man touched by God, who lived
in the world with a heart on fire with love."

IRVIN SERRANO PHOTOGRAPHY

David C. Weiss is a writer whose poems reflect his experience of the Divine and invite readers to travel a path that can lead them to discover the Divine within themselves. He is a presenter, workshop leader, and consultant in the areas of spiritual growth and group development. He is a student of the *shakuhachi,* a Japanese bamboo flute played in Zen meditation. He has a master's degree in theology and a doctorate in pastoral psychology from Boston University. He practiced for thirty-five years as a Licensed Marriage and Family Therapist in the Boston and Portland, Maine, areas, and now spends part of the year teaching poetry to Tibetan Buddhist monks at Sera Jhy Monastic University in South India, where one of his sons is a Buddhist monk. His other son is a teacher in the Boston area.